MARQUETRY AND VENEERS

MARQUETRY
AND VENEERS

By
EDWARD KITSON

W. & G. FOYLE, LTD.
119-125, CHARING CROSS ROAD, LONDON, W.C.2

First published 1951
Reprinted June, 1952

PRINTED IN GREAT BRITAIN BY
EBENEZER BAYLIS AND SON, LTD., THE
TRINITY PRESS, WORCESTER, AND LONDON

CONTENTS

5

INTRODUCTION

MARQUETRY is a method of enriching or decorating articles, usually of wood, by cutting the separate parts of a prepared design to shape, and assembling the pieces by glueing them to the foundation article. The materials most often used for this work are thin veneers of wood, although other materials may be used.

The craft of marquetry has a long history, and in order to appreciate the modern scope of interest, it is necessary to know something of the growth and development of the craft.

Marquetry as we know it to-day, originated from Inlay, which is a method of decoration effected by the inlaying or insertion of one material into another material, contrasting in colour and composition. For Inlay, such materials as metal, wood, stone, marble, and ivory are used; also shell, as in the case of mother-of-pearl inlay, which is worked with polished pieces of pearl-oyster shell. In the fourteenth century, Italian workers used bone and ivory extensively for their fine Inlay work, and in the fifteenth century, stone and marble were used for mosaic work.

In Inlay, the shaped materials are sunken into the ground, and finished flush with surrounding surfaces. The term "inlay" is often used to describe marquetry, which is really a development of Inlay.

True marquetry is also a development of Intarsia or Tarsia, which is a form of wood mosaic, employing dyed and stained woods. In the sixteenth and seventeenth centuries, German and Italian craftsmen used Intarsia for the decoration of furniture. Marquetry—although allied to Intarsia and Inlay—was also practised as a separate craft by continental craftsmen for the enrichment of furniture.

Marquetry in tortoiseshell, metal and ebony, was developed in France during the seventeenth century by André Charles Boulle. In England, marquetry in fine wood was introduced by continental craftsmen and was copied—not very successfully at first—by English workers. Arabesque or seaweed marquetry which was used largely for enriching clock cases, became very popular, but it later suffered a decline, largely due, no doubt, to our quarrels with the French.

7

In the eighteenth century, marquetry was again popular for enriching cabinets, clock cases, caskets and other articles of furniture, and later a form of pictorial or "picture" marquetry was developed, in which veneers were used to "paint" pictures in wood. John Ruskin condemned these wood-painted pictures, but they continued to enjoy some measure of popularity, and recently this form of marquetry has undergone a revival of interest.

The picture marquetry is now a modern craft, and it is widely practised as a specialized branch of the parent craft. This is largely due to the fact that very few tools and little equipment are required, also that parcels of quite small pieces of a very wide range of veneers are obtainable at low cost, in relation to their use and purpose.

It should be appreciated that marquetry and veneering are two distinct and separate crafts, although the common materials in both crafts are wood veneers. Marquetry is a form of work in which pieces of veneers are shaped, to be assembled and affixed to a solid basis, in the manner—to use a very broad comparison—as a jig-saw puzzle is assembled. In this work, the colours, grains and natural markings of the veneers are used to their best advantage, as will be explained later in full detail.

Veneering, as separate from marquetry, consists of glueing sheets of veneer on bases of more common woods, but it must be stressed that veneering is not a cheap shoddy way of covering poor materials and indifferent workmanship, with thin layers of expensive woods, although there have been many abuses of this method of finishing. It should also be appreciated that not all woods from which richly decorated veneers are obtained, are suitable for use in the solid, in making pieces of furniture.

Veneered work is a happy marriage of two—or more—complementary woods, in which the standard of workmanship of the foundation structure is equal to that of the overlaid work. Another point for consideration is the scarcity of finely marked and figured timbers from which veneers are cut.

The craft of veneering has a long and interesting history, but this book deals with the separate craft of marquetry, in which veneers are used, and the history of veneering is not dealt with here. The emphasis in this book is on marquetry, in its popular modern form of pictorial or picture marquetry, and I am indebted to Messrs Handicrafts, Ltd., of Peterborough for their kindness in supplying detailed information on veneers for pictorial marquetry.

This branch of the craft is described in very great detail in the following instructions, which include a wealth of information about veneering.

Pictorial marquetry can be made a complete pastime, which can be worked for pleasure and profit. It can be made a craft that shows a good return on the expenditure of time and materials. Picture marquetry is a craft of artistic invention, which provides full interest.

CHAPTER I

Veneers — methods of production — qualities, selection and conversion. **Saw-cut Veneers:** How produced — identification — preparation — flitches — machine cutting — wastage — costs. **Flat Slicing:** Advantages — method of cutting — steaming — slicing, clipping and drying. **Rotary Cutting:** "Peeling" — steaming and turning — processing — thicknesses. **Half Rotary Cutting:** Sectional cutting — purpose. **Varieties:** Types of wood — selection — terms.

BEFORE commencing the work of preparing and making a marquetry picture, it is necessary to know something about the main materials—veneers—and how they are produced. Veneers are known by the name of the wood from which they are produced, and by the processes employed in cutting them. In some cases, there are different varieties of each wood, and these will be described in detail later. The main methods of cutting veneers are saw cutting, rotary cutting, and knife cutting; another method is known as half rotary cutting.

In the production of veneers, experienced selection is made of the wood, and also of the method used for converting the selected woods into veneers. Inferior qualities of veneers are usually the result of wrong methods used in the preliminary stages, and the best veneers are produced by manufacturers of experience, who are equipped to apply the conversion methods best suited to individual types of wood.

SAW-CUT VENEERS

Saw-cut veneer is the thickest kind which, as its name implies, is produced by cutting the wood with a saw into thin slices. In this form of preparation, there is considerable waste, as much of the wood is converted into sawdust. Saw-cut veneers may be identified from the saw marks on each side of the thin sheet of wood.

The method of producing saw-cut veneers is illustrated in Fig. 1. Usually, the log of wood is cut into "flitches", which is the term used to describe squared pieces of timber. Also, the log may be sawn into thin sheets, after first cutting it lengthwise, through

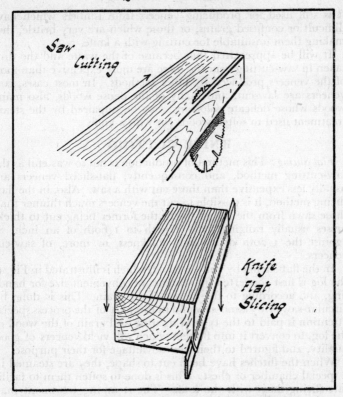

Fig. I. FLAT-CUTTING VENEERS

the centre. Saw cutting is the oldest method of producing veneers. A special circular saw is used, and the setting is different from that of other types of saws. Great skill is necessary to work this method successfully.

The flitches, or the logs, are mounted on a travelling carriage, which moves along a fixed track to the revolving saw. After each veneer is cut, the flitch or log is moved across the saw, to the thickness required for the next veneer to be cut, plus an allowance for the width of the kerf. This very old method of producing veneers has now been largely superseded by more modern methods, but it is still used for producing veneers from timbers which have difficult or confused grains, or those which are very brittle, thus making them unsuitable for cutting with a knife.

It will be appreciated that because of the waste and the time taken in saw-cutting veneers, these are more expensive than most of the veneers produced by other methods. In most cases, curl veneers are saw-cut, and many of the dense woods, also many woods whose delicate colouring may be impaired by the steam treatment used to soften woods cut with a knife.

KNIFE CUTTING

Flat Slicing : This method of production is not so wasteful as the saw-cutting method, and consequently, flat-sliced veneers are usually less expensive than those cut with a saw. Also, in the flat-slicing method, it is possible to cut the veneers much thinner than those sawn from the log or flitch, the former being cut to thicknesses usually ranging from 1/30th to 1/60th of an inch, as against the 1/20th of an inch thickness, or more, of saw-cut veneers.

In the flat-slicing by knife method, which is illustrated in Fig. 1, the log is first converted into flitches of convenient size for handling, and according to the nature of the grain. This is done by circular-saw or by band-saw and in this part of the process special attention is paid to the type of figuring and grain of the wood of the log, to convert it into flitches which will yield veneers of good quality, and figured to their best advantage for their purpose.

When the flitches have been cut to shape, they are steamed in a special chamber or chest. This is done to soften them to facilitate slicing them with the knife. The steaming treatment may vary according to the type of wood, depending on the characteristic of each individual timber; usually the flitches are steamed for twelve hours.

In the veneer-slicing process, the flitch is fastened or "dogged" to a bed, which forms the body of the machine. The knife is positioned to slice diagonally across the grain, to remove a sheet or "leaf" of veneer each time the knife completes a stroke. The action is similar to planing a piece of wood, except that the veneer is usually sliced across the grain of the wood, and in planing, the shaving is taken off with the grain. As the sheets of veneer are cut, they are placed together in the order of cutting, which permits good matching. This is essential in furniture making.

After cutting, the sliced veneers or leaves are trimmed or "clipped" to size, and they are then dried. This is an important part of the process of production, which is done very carefully. Unless the heat is applied evenly all over the sheet, contraction may take place, causing cracks and splits. Veneers are usually machine-dried, by passing them over steam-heated rollers or plates, or they may be dried by heated air on moving bands. After flattening any cockled sheets the veneers are stored flat in a dry place, which should be dimly lit, and in which the temperature is controlled.

The reaction of veneers to light varies according to the nature of the timber. Some woods tend to darken—others bleach on exposure to strong light.

Rotary Cutting: This is the third main method of producing veneers, which is sometimes known as "peeling". This is illustrated in Fig. 2, and this method of cutting is also used in the production of plywoods.

In this method, the log is not cut into flitches. After it has been trimmed and steamed, the log is fitted into a machine which rotates—rather in the manner of a large lathe. As the log is turned, a long knife, which is firmly mounted on a heavy carriage, "peels" or cuts a continuous slice of wood from the log. The action of the knife is so adjusted that the blade moves inwards, to ensure that the veneer is cut to an even thickness. As this veneer is peeled from the log, it passes to another machine which cuts or clips it into sizes convenient to handle. From there, the veneer goes through the process of drying, previously described.

Generally, veneers cut by this method are not so well marked as those cut by other methods, and the flat-sliced veneers are generally considered superior to those produced by rotary cutting. Veneers which are rotary cut, may be produced in thicknesses ranging from 3/8ths of an inch, to 1/80th of an inch, and some machines are capable of cutting even thinner veneers— some to 1/120th of an inch—depending on the quality and characteristics of the wood, and the purpose for which the veneer is to be used. The knife carriages are geared to regulate the thickness of the peel.

Half Rotary Cutting: This method, as its name implies, is similar to full rotary cutting, where a complete log is revolved against a knife, except that in half rotary cutting, only a section of the log is

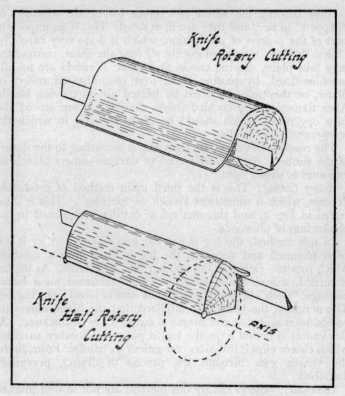

Fig. 2. ROTARY-CUTTING VENEERS

revolved against the knife. The method is illustrated in Fig. 2.
In half rotary cutting, the wood is peeled into leaves, instead of a
continuous strip. This method is used with certain types of wood,
to produce finely marked and figured veneers.

VARIETIES

Veneers may be produced from all the woods used in cabinet
making, and in addition, from many other woods not usually
used in bulk as cabinet-making woods.

Veneers for cabinet making cannot be produced from every log of wood, but only from selected logs of a certain standard of quality. The age and condition of the wood has also to be taken into consideration. Many of the woods are rare and are much sought after.

A list of the main varieties of veneers is given in a following chapter. This is by no means complete, but it includes those used by the pictorial marquetry working, and provides a good range of colourings.

In addition to the colour of the veneer, and the name of the parent wood, some varieties are identified by their markings such as straight-grains, burrs, butts and curls—being special figurings. These terms are explained in the next chapter.

CHAPTER II

Figuring — formation. **Burrs:** How formed — handling. **Butts:** Formation and description. **Curls:** Feather markings — sizes. **Roe:** Description. Storing veneers — veneers for pictorial marquetry.

In addition to knowing something about the production of veneers, the marquetry worker should know the meaning of the terms used to describe certain veneer figurings.

Figuring in some timbers is due to the disposition of the tissue of the medullary rays, but in most woods the medullary rays are not responsible for the figuring. The grain is the true wood fibre which is seen as the annular rings. Figuring, in many cases, is due to the crossing of the medullary rays and the annular rings; and the direction of the knife or saw in cutting logs and flitches across the undulating of the grain, is responsible for the revelation of the figuring.

The figuring of some woods is due to the out-growing of branches and roots, and sometimes to disease and deformities of the tree. The main terms used to describe types of figuring are given below.

Burrs: These are caused by excrescences of wart-like growths on the outside of the trunk of a tree. They are really deformities, but they provide the figuring of some very attractive veneers— such as in the case of Italian walnut, cherry, ash and amboyna, etc. The figuring of burrs is small (see the illustration, Fig. 3), and is composed of numerous small knots grouped closely together. Unless burrs are carefully handled in cutting and using the veneers, small hard parts tend to break away.

Butts: This term is used to describe veneers which are cut across the stump or butt of a tree, and the characteristic figuring is due to the growth of the root. Butts are similar to curls, described below.

Curls: This is a term used to describe the characteristic markings, which are also known as feathers, formed at the junctions of large branches with the trunk of a tree. This is illustrated in Fig. 4. The curls, or feathers, vary greatly in shape and size, according to the formation of the junction of branch and trunk.

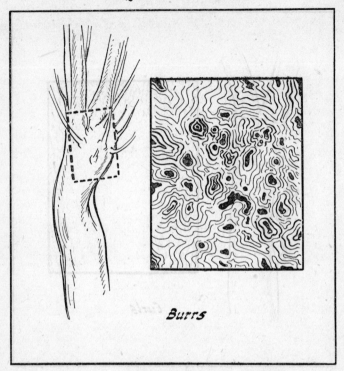

Burrs

Fig. 3. FORMATION OF BURRS

This form of figuring is common to walnut, although it may be found in other varieties of veneer.

Roe : This term is used to describe the formation of dark flecks, due to grain fibres, twisting round a tree.

Most of the terms described have more significance in cabinet making than in pictorial marquetry, although they have their uses and purposes, as will be explained later in the instructions.

Veneers need careful handling and storing. Most of them are brittle to some extent; this varies according to the variety. When purchasing veneers, the surface of both sides should be carefully examined, to ensure that the wood has been cleanly cut, and that there are no irregularities due to torn fibres.

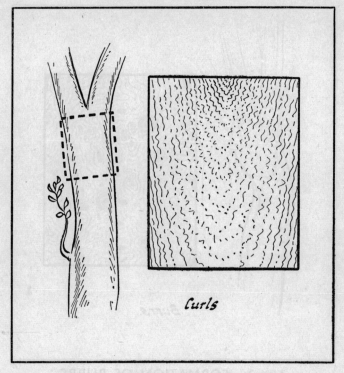

Curls

Fig. 4.   FORMATION OF CURLS

All veneers should be stored in a humid atmosphere, flat on shelves, or otherwise suitably supported, between two boards. It is best to obtain a sufficient quantity of a particular type of veneer for the work in hand, as there may be some slight differences of colouring and markings in woods of the same type, also because of the scarcity of some woods. The marquetry picture maker will be able to purchase quantities of veneer of mixed varieties in small parcels, and usually these parcels of veneers are extremely good value for money.

In pictorial marquetry there should be little or no waste, and a good use can be found for every small piece.

Before going on to describe tools and working methods, it is necessary to provide some information about the varieties of veneers. These are described in the following chapter, and the veneers are listed in alphabetical order, under the names by which they are most widely known. It should be appreciated that some woods have several different names, but in the following list the varieties are listed under their main names.

The colours of the veneers are given, but the picture marquetry worker should see actual specimens of the woods, before planning a picture.

CHAPTER III

Different varieties of wood veneers.

THIS chapter is devoted to descriptions of the different varieties of wood veneers, which include details of colourings, markings, and in most cases the country of origin. Many of them are scarce and may not be easy to obtain, but the variety is so great that the marquetry picture maker should have little difficulty in finding a substitute, if the first choice is not obtainable.

Acacia: A warm rich brown in colour, with a bold dark grain, and usually well figured. From France; there is also an Australian variety, which is light crimson in colour, and is boldly marked.

Acajou: A yellowish-brown veneer, marked with reddish bands. A member of the cedar family; mostly from Eastern countries.

Amboyna Burr: Reddish-to-golden-brown in colour, with a rich close burr. Some varieties are strongly streaked, and the burrs, which are usually small and irregular in shape, are beautifully marked and figured. Mostly from Borneo.

Ash: Obtainable in colours ranging from white to pinkish straw. Has a coarse, uninteresting grain, although some species are richly mottled. Sometimes marred by small black knots. From Europe and Japan.

Banksia: Light buff in colour, with a beautiful grain. From Western Australia.

Black Bean: A rich medium-brown in colour. Usually brittle, and may be found difficult to cut. Has a strongly marked grain, which is somewhat like walnut. Australian in origin, from New South Wales.

Blackwood: This wood ranges from greenish-black to brown in colour, and is a variety of ebony. From the West Indies.

Birch: There are several varieties of birch; Masur or Curly is white to cream in colour, marked with clusters of black flecks, and has bright figuring in heavy waves. From Eastern Europe.

Birch: (Canadian White or Silkywood). Also known as Betula. Has large figuring, and is obtainable in white or dark pink (heartwood). From Canada.

Boxwood : A light yellow in colour. Is hard, with a dense grain, but has no figure. From Asia and Europe.

Bubinga : A purplish-red in colour. This is a beautiful wood, which has strong figuring. (Is sometimes known as African Rosewood.) Comes from West Africa.

Cedar : A light brownish-red in colour. Very similar in appearance to Honduras Mahogany. A soft wood, which is easily worked. Is pleasantly figured and has a fragrant smell. Mostly from Honduras.

Cherrywood : (Nigerian). This is a reddish-brown wood, with a colour similar to that of Mahogany. It is often marked with a heavy black mottle. It is a very beautiful wood. This variety of Cherrywood comes from West Africa.

Cherrywood : (Pacific). The colour is a soft shade of salmon pink. It is a very hard wood, marked with tight burrs, which are evenly distributed. This variety of Cherrywood comes from the Pacific Coast.

Chestnut : This is light brown in colour, with little or no figures. From European countries.

Cocus : This wood varies, from greenish-black to brown in colour, and it is a variety of ebony, which is found in the West Indies.

Cormandel : This wood, which is similar to Macassar Ebony, is black in colour, and it is marked with wide streaks of light colourings, from pink to grey. It is a hard wood, which comes from Africa.

Courbaril : This is a gay wood, with a background of old gold, marked with black and brown irregular streaks, and it comes from Guiana and the West Indies.

Ebony : (Macassar). Macassar Ebony is a hard wood, which is streaked with black and light pink marks. It is a difficult wood to work, and it is only supplied in narrow widths. This comes from the Celebes Island.

Elm : This varies in colour, from reddish-brown to green. It has a wild curly grain and it comes from Europe.

Greywood : (Birds-eye and Harewood). The veneer from this wood is silver grey in colour with a bright sheen. It is a variety of maple and sycamore, which are chemically treated, to give the grey effect. From Canada and Europe.

Greywood : (Indian Silver). This is brownish-grey to green in colour, which is marked with brown irregular streaks. It is a handsome timber, which comes from India.

Holly : White in colour, and is considered to be the whitest wood in existence. It has practically no grain but it is very hard. Holly is a European wood.

Jarrah : This is a dull brownish brick red colour. It is a very close-textured wood, with some mottled markings. It is very hard and is uninteresting. From Australia.

Kamassi : This wood is a light yellow in colour. It is hard, with a very close grain. Comes from South Africa.

Karri : Dull brown in colour, and marked with wavy figurings. From Western Australia.

Kauri : This is a light reddish brown wood, mottled with pleasing figuring. It is a variety of pine, from New Zealand.

Kingwood : A rich violet brown in colour, streaked with golden yellow. This is a hard brittle wood, which is only obtainable in small pieces. From Brazil.

Lacewood : (Planetree). This wood has a pale reddish colour. It is cut radially, and has a fine silver grain. It is very attractive. From European countries.

Lauan : A light brown to dark reddish brown wood, with a silky lustre, which comes from the Philippines.

Laurel : Dark greyish brown in colour, with black streaks and often figured with a rich mottle. This is a dark handsome wood, which comes from India.

Lime : This is a light yellowish white in colour, with a close even grain, from India and West Indies.

Madrona : Coloured a warm pink red. A beautiful wood, with a rich burr. From North America.

Mahogany : There are several varieties of this wood, which is described as the king of woods. It is mainly pale red in colour. Blistered cherry, striped and quilted, from West Africa. A fiddleback variety, well marked, is found in Honduras, but the finest curls are considered to come from Cuba. It is a delightful wood to work.

Maidu : (Also known as "false" or "mock" Amboyna). This is a reddish wood. It is less brittle than Amboyna and is marked with burrs. From Borneo.

Makori : Colour varies from light pink to red. There is also a variety of French Cherrywood, called Makori. West Africa.

Maple: (Birds-eye). White to cream in colour, with masses of "eyes". From Canada.

Maple: (Quilted). White to cream in colour, with a heavy quilted grain. Also from Canada.

Maple: (Queensland). Reddish brown in colour. The butts show a brilliant mottle. It has a hard surface, but it is easily worked. From Australia.

Morrell: A warm red brown in colour. A faint grain. Has good figuring. Comes from the eucalyptus family. From Australia.

Myrtle: (Burrs). White to grey in colour, with a greenish tint. Well marked with good burrs. From the Pacific Coast.

Oak: There are many varieties of oak, such as brown figured and silky. The English variety is considered to be the best. Brown oak is rich in colour, and is handsomely marked, but is rather brittle. English figured oak is cream to brown in colour, and is richest in silver grain. Although figured oaks are European in origin, and are finer in texture and colour, being whiter than the English variety, the American figured oak is darker in colour than the European variety, which is redder and more coarse in texture. There is Japanese oak, which is darker than the other oaks, being brown in colour and, being a mild wood, it is easily worked. Another variety of oak is known as silky oak, and is pink to red in colour, with a coarse silver grain. This variety comes from Queensland.

Obeche: A straw-coloured wood, which has a coarse grain. It is light in weight and is soft. Obeche is from Nigeria.

Olive Ash: This wood has a white ground, with brown markings. It is usually marked and often has a wild grain. From European countries and North America.

Padauk: (Andaman). A rich crimson in colour, with no outstanding figure. From the Andaman Islands.

Padauk: (Burmese). A reddish brown wood, which is sometimes richly mottled. From Burma.

Pear: Varies in colour, from pinkish brown to straw. Has a close grain, and is found in many countries, but mostly European.

Peroba: A pale golden olive to cinnamon in colour, with wild figures or mottles. A brittle wood, which comes from Brazil.

Poplar: Whitish yellow in colour, with a green tinge. A soft wood, from European countries.

Purpleheart: As its name implies, this is purple in colour and is generally even in tone. It is close grained, but has no figure. From Brazil.

Red Gum: A dark reddish brown in colour, with a watered figure. From Southern Australia.

Redwood: (Sequoia). This is a brick red to brown colour. Varies with burrs and figures, which are often very beautiful. It is a soft wood, which may be found difficult to work. From California.

Rewa: This has a silvery colour, and it is marked with figures. Similar to Lacewood. From New Zealand.

Rimo: Deep red in colour, with dark markings. With burrs and finely figured. A variety of red pine, from New Zealand.

Rosewood: (Indian). Purple in colour, with pale reddish brown streaks. From India.

Rosewood: (Rio). Reddish in colour, with dark purple brown to black markings. Has a striking figure. Cracks easily. Is from Brazil.

Saffron Wood: Straw colour and is closely grained, with a good figure. From South Africa.

Satine: A deep brown red in colour. Lustrous, with a good figure. From Guiana.

Satinwood: Golden yellow in colour, with beautiful mottle. A hard wood from India.

Snake Wood: Dark chestnut colour, with mottled bands, from British Guiana.

Sycamore: White to cream in colour, with strong fiddle-back markings. There is a weathered variety of sycamore, which is light brown to pinkish beige in colour. Both varieties are found in England.

Teak: Olive brown in colour, often pleasantly mottled. From Burma.

Thuya: (Burrs). Dark reddish brown in colour. Strongly marked with rich burrs. A very hard wood, from North America.

Toon: Pale red in colour. Straight grained wood. From Burma.

Tulipwood: A straw-coloured ground, with broad red markings. It is an oily wood, which is hard, and it is supplied in narrow billets. From Brazil.

Violet Wood: A dark purple in colour, with darker streaks. It is a hard close-grained wood. It is found in Guiana and South America.

Walnut: (American). A fairly uniform purplish brown colour.

Sometimes highly figured, but generally plain. From North America.

Walnut : (Brazilian). Brown to olive green in colour. A very hard wood. It is handsome in appearance. From Brazil.

Walnut : (English). Grey to brown colouring, with black markings. Found in England.

Walnut : (French and Italian). Has dark brown to black markings on a grey ground. Often richly figured. The source of some of the finest burrs and butts. From France and Italy.

Walnut : (Queensland). Dark grey in colour, with heavy mottle. From Australia.

Willow : (Burrs). Pinkish brown in colour, strongly marked with burrs, which are often spoilt by small black brittle knots. Found in England.

Yew : A rich warm brown colour with burrs. Resembles Thuya, and is rather scarce. Found in Europe and Asia.

Zebra Wood : Is red brown in colour, with dark stripes. From Brazil.

Zebrona : A ground of buff to yellow, with dark brown to black streaks, usually running in parallel lines. From West Africa.

CHAPTER IV

Materials, Equipment and Tools: Veneers — mounting boards — adhesives — working surface — saw table — knives — saw and blades. **Designs:** Suitable designs — use of figuring — landscapes and buildings — adapting pictures — example of method — colourings — selection of veneers — styles of work — enlarging designs — fitness of work.

MATERIALS, EQUIPMENT AND TOOLS

THE main materials—veneers—have been described in the previous chapter. Others required are, mounting boards for the marquetry pictures (described more fully in later chapters), and some glue or cement. For large work, ordinary Scotch glue thinned with water may be used, and for small work or practice pieces, a good universal cement, such as Samson, is suitable for use.

The amount and variety of equipment required will vary with the class of work being done. For general purposes, the marquetry picture worker will require a flat solid bench top or table, on which to do the work of preparation and assembly. The veneer may be cut on the bench top or on a working board, which is perhaps best. The working board may be wood, glass or zinc. It should be perfectly smooth and free from any holes, nails or screw-heads, etc., which may cause the thin veneers to split, or otherwise damage them. For most purposes, a glass or zinc working board will be found best—although wood may be used, there is a danger that the knife used for cutting the veneers may tend to "wander" and be guided by the grain of the wood, and so spoil a piece of work.

Another general piece of equipment required is a small cutting table, which can be clamped to a work bench or table. A fretwork cutting table, with "v" notch, as illustrated in Fig. 5, is suitable for use when cutting veneers.

The main tool required is a really sharp knife with a pointed blade, and some veneer-cutting knives are illustrated in Fig 6. Small-bladed craft knives and stencil knives are also suitable for cutting veneers. Some workers prefer to use a stiff razor blade for cutting, and some of the woods may be cut with scissors, al-

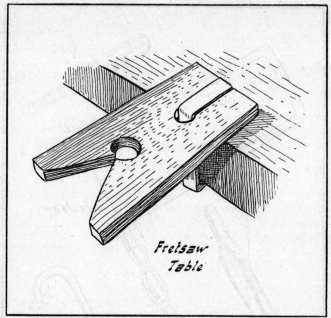

Fretsaw
Table

Fig. 5.   TABLE DEVICE FOR CUTTING

though this is not recommended as a general method. As with other crafts, the pictorial marquetry worker will develop methods of his own, and use the tools best suited to his individual style.

A small saw will be required, and a frame of the type illustrated in Fig. 6 is suitable for cutting the thin wood veneers. With the saw frame will be required some very fine-toothed saw blades. Another useful tool is a pair of tweezers for handling small shaped pieces of brittle veneers. Some strong "G" cramps—four should be enough—will be required, also some miscellaneous tools and items of equipment which are to be found in most craftworkers' work rooms, such as pencils, a rule, glass-paper, etc., will be required. These tools and equipment are sufficient for the beginner to commence with, and other tools, etc., required for more advanced forms of work will be mentioned in the chapters describing their uses.

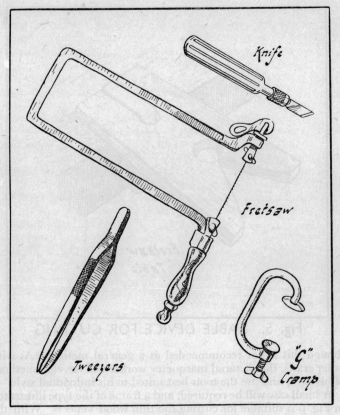

Fig. 6. MARQUETRY TOOLS

DESIGNS

For pictorial marquetry, bold clear designs with large pattern features should be used—small-featured intricate designs are not entirely suitable, and these are out of keeping with the true character of the craft. The best effects are gained by using the grains and wood markings to their best advantage, to create a natural appearance of life. To give a simple example: if the marquetry picture was of a Tudor period house with timbered walls, a dark coloured straight-grained veneer with small markings would be suitable for the beams, with a lighter coloured wood, devoid of strong markings, used to represent the plastered walls. This, of course, is a very elementary example, and the treatment of each picture is a matter for careful consideration in the selection and uses of the different types of veneers—but more of this later.

The most suitable designs for pictorial marquetry are those depicting landscapes or buildings. Figures of people and animals may be included, but these should be shown in outline or silhouette, rather than to attempt to define their features.

Pictorial marquetry designs are best adapted from existing pictures—prints or photographs, and in most cases it will be necessary to modify some of the outlines and details to make the picture-designs suitable for the class of work. To illustrate this in a simple way, a picture is shown in Fig. 7. It is a landscape scene of a cottage, near the side of a road, with sloping ground each side, and some trees and bushes, with a cloudy sky. This was drawn from a photograph and, as it is, contains rather too much small detail for use as a marquetry picture.

The illustration, Fig. 8, shows how the detailed picture has been altered, to make it suitable for use as a pictorial marquetry design for the beginner. The wispy clouds have been omitted in the new drawing, and the main outlines have been made bolder, without losing any of the essential features necessary to make a good picture. The shape of the bushes in the right foreground have been changed, to make them more effective, and the cottage outlines have been strengthened to define them more clearly.

The trees, too, have undergone some small changes to give them cleaner outlines, and all this has been done to retain depth and perspective, so necessary to a pictorial scene of this nature.

So far, so good. The picture is now transformed into a suitable design for pictorial marquetry with black outlines on a white ground. To assist in the selection of appropriate veneers, the outline picture can be coloured with water colours, keeping the colouring bold and simple, and essentially natural.

At this stage, after colouring the picture, the veneers may be selected, choosing them first for appropriate colourings, the second consideration being the figuring of the woods. It is in this part of the work that the artist in wood can achieve beauty and

Fig. 7. PICTURE BEFORE ADAPTING

perfection in his craft, by taking full advantage of the grain formations, and such features as burrs and curls.

In the example illustrated in Fig. 8, the grain of the wood chosen to represent the sky, should run across the picture, from side to side. The grain figuring should not be too strong, or the colour of the wood too dark. The piece of veneer cut to represent the road, would be best selected with light grain markings, running the longest way of the road. It may be possible for this piece of the picture to find a piece of veneer with the grain figuring gradually merging at the end of the road, thus providing depth of perspective. These, of course, are very simple examples, and the selection of woods most suitable for their purpose will be dealt with more fully later in the book.

It will be appreciated, from the points mentioned above, that many types of pictures may be adapted for pictorial marquetry, provided they can be simplified if the detail is small, to suit individual styles of work. Of course, like every other craft, the possibilities and limitations of the materials and working methods

Fig. 8. PICTURE ADAPTED

can only fully be appreciated after practice, and it is necessary in this craft of pictorial marquetry to be practical in applying the knowledge gained in the early stages.

No amount of words in a book can make the marquetry worker a skilled craftsman; it is necessary to gain skill in action.

The simple example illustrated in Fig. 8 may be used as a practice design, or an existing print or photograph may be adapted for use as a practice design. Magazine illustrations provide a good source of inspiration, and designs may easily be enlarged or reduced. This is done by drawing pencil lines on the original design, or to make a good tracing of it, to divide it into squares. To enlarge the design, a sheet of paper should also be lined to form squares as large as required, and with the same number of squares as the original. With this done, the outlines of the details in the squares of the original, should be drawn in the larger squares, faithfully repeating each part of the original drawing.

It is best for the design paper to be white in colour, and as it may have to be handled many times during the making of a picture, it should not be flimsy. In the perfection of a craft, no detail in the preliminary stages is too trivial for consideration. Even the careful selection of design paper is important. In many cases, beginners to a new craft are rather inclined to rush through the preparatory stages, to achieve the satisfaction of accomplishment. It is a good thing to be enthusiastic, but always there must be a careful and practical approach to the work in hand.

In designing a marquetry picture, the artistic is allied to the practical, and the completed work is essentially the product of the individual.

CHAPTER V

Transferring Designs: Use of carbon paper — accuracy in marking out — "Pouncing" — method — use of oiled paper — making a pricking tool — pouncing with bitumen powder — making a dabber — fixing the powder — other methods — selection of veneers — multiple cutting — saw-rag waste. **Cutting:** Table and saw — cutting straight lines and simple outline shapes.

TRANSFERRING DESIGNS

THERE are several ways of transferring or marking the outline shapes of pieces of a wood picture, to the veneers. The most obvious method is one that employs the use of carbon paper, although with care, outline shapes may be marked on veneers with carbon paper, and this method may be used for cutting odd pieces, it is not advisable to regard it as the best or only method.

The work of marking the selected timbers to shape, requires care. If marking out is not done accurately, no amount of care in cutting, assembly, and finishing, will make it a good picture. Each shaped part must fit perfectly to its neighbour and, although it is possible to remove any extra wood to ensure good fitting, gaps and joining edges cannot be filled—they can be patched up, of course; but this is not good marquetry.

The use of carbon paper may encourage inaccuracies. The thickness of the design paper, carbon paper and tracing paper tends to thicken outlines, and unless a very sharp hard pencil is used, the outlines of the parts may be thicker in some places than in others. Also, in carboning outlines directly on to the wood, there is a tendency for the pencil point to "wander" with the grain of the wood. It may be found also that some types of carbon paper will smudge and mark the wood. The object in cutting the parts to shape, is to cut them accurately, so that each piece fits perfectly into place, and the best method of ensuring accuracy in marking design outlines, is to "pounce" the design.

"Pouncing" is a term used to describe the outlining of design shapes with black powder, applied through pin-holes in the design paper line. The method of procedure is as follows. First,

the design should be drawn or traced full size on paper of a substantial quality. (If the craft is to be practised as a commercial
venture, oiled parchment paper, as used for covering lampshades,
will be found best for use, as the design may be stored after the
picture is completed, and be used again at any time in the future,
over and over again.) The pencil lines should be firm and narrow,
and when all the design has been marked on the paper, the work
of pricking can be commenced.

For pricking holes in the design paper, a simple tool can be
made. This consists of a needle and a short length of dowel rod.
The needle should be inserted through one end of the rod, which
forms the handle, as illustrated in Fig. 9. Lay the design paper
over a piece of thick cardboard then, with the pricker tool, go
over all the lines of the design, including the edge outlines. Make
the holes as close together as possible. This may be found rather

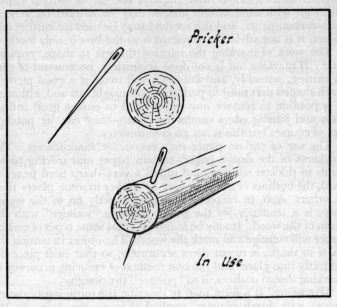

Fig. 9. MAKING A PRICKER

a tedious job, but the time spent can be considered a wise invest-
ment. Pay special attention to corners and to any intricately
shaped edges. A straight edge may be used as a guide, to assist in
pricking straight lines. The small holes should be pricked cleanly
through the paper, and exactly on the pencilled lines.

The next part of the work consists of the actual process of
pouncing, which is done with bitumen powder. Each part of the
design should be pounced separately on a different piece of paper.
One end of the design paper should be clipped to a flat piece of
wood or stout cardboard, and the transfer paper should be placed
in position between the board and design paper and held firmly
in place while the powder is being used. The powder should be
kept in a tin or jar with airtight closure. Only a very little of the
powder is used at a time, and for pouncing a design, a small
amount should be tipped into a shallow container.

A small dabber will be required for pouncing, and this can be
made from a piece of wood, by covering one end with felt or
chamois leather, as illustrated in Fig. 10. The padding material
should be firmly attached to the wooden handle, by winding
string round the ends of the material and tying it tightly.

To transfer the design outlines to the pattern paper, the end
of the padded tool should be dipped in the bitumen powder, then
tapped on the lines of the design part, replenishing the powder on
the pad, as necessary. Lightly dab over all the pricked outlines
of the shape being transferred, and before removing the transfer
paper, lift the design paper and inspect the work, to ensure that
all the outlines are firm and clear. Any surplus powder on the
design paper should be tipped back into the container for re-use.

The powder tapped through the pricked holes in the design
paper on to the transfer paper, will be loose, but no attempt
should be made to tip any surplus back into the container. The
powdered pattern paper should be handled very carefully until
the powder is fixed. To do this, hold the paper with the pattern
uppermost over the flame of a spirit lamp, or if it is a large piece
of paper, over a gas ring. The paper should not be permitted to
ignite, and as soon as it commences scorching, it should be
removed from the flame. This heating will fix the powdered
outlines, which cannot afterwards be rubbed off.

A pattern should be made for each separate part of the design,
in the manner described above.

This method of pouncing has been described in great detail,

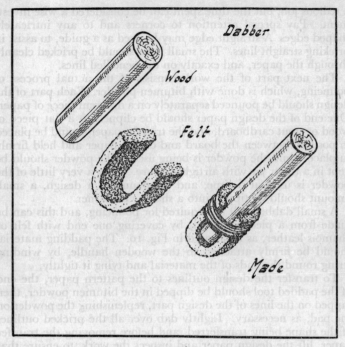

Dabber

Wood

Felt

Made

Fig. 10. MAKING A DABBER

for the benefit of the complete beginner and it is, in the writer's opinion, the most reliable one for the pictorial marquetry worker. Of course, other methods may be used to suit the working style of the individual. There are some workers who swear by the carbon paper method of transferring designs, and one worker of the writer's acquaintance uses embroidery transfers, which he says are ideal for large work, such as firescreens. Each worker will, no doubt, use the method best suited to his own way of working.

After all the parts of the design have been transferred, the transfer papers should be affixed to the selected veneers. These, of course, are chosen to use the natural characteristics of the woods to their best advantage and, as previously described, selection can be facilitated by colouring the original design. It should be appreciated that there is some restriction in the use of colour, most veneers being red, brown, yellow and green in colour, although there are many shades of most of these colours.

After selecting the veneers for the picture, the transfer paper should be affixed to the thin sheets of wood. Glue, very thinly mixed, may be used as the adhesive. The glued paper should be positioned on the veneer, with the grain running in the required direction. The paper should be smoothed flat on the wood, and care should be taken not to stretch it. When the glue has chilled and set, the parts are ready for cutting to shape. If only one picture is to be made, the pattern shapes may be cut singly, but if the craft is to be practised as a commercial venture, the parts for several pictures can be cut at the same time. The selected veneers should be placed together with grain markings all running in the same direction. The pieces should then be held together with small veneer pins, and the points of the pins should be nipped off, to prevent splitting the thin veneer. The pins, of course, should be positioned in the waste and not inside the design outlines, and when this has been done, the parts may be cut to shape, see Fig. 11. The bottom piece of veneer should be an odd piece which, because of the saw-rag, will be cut to waste, or a thin piece of common wood—such as three-ply—may be positioned under the layers of the veneers. This saw-rag wastage also applies if only one piece of veneer is being cut at a time.

CUTTING

For cutting, a very fine-toothed fretsaw blade should be used— the finest obtainable, and when cutting the veneers, which should be held firmly on the "v" cutting table, the saw blade must be kept perfectly upright. If this is not done, the sawn edge will slope, and if several pieces of veneer are cut at the same time, there may be quite a lot of difference in the sizes of the top and bottom pieces. Also, unless the cut edges are square, the picture pieces will not fit closely together.

The object in cutting the pieces to shape, is to cut them to the *exact* size required. At first, this may be found difficult to do, and the shaped pieces may require trimming at the edges, but as the worker acquires skill in practice, the aim should be to cut each

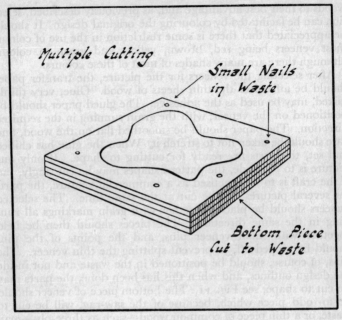

Multiple Cutting

Small Nails in Waste

Bottom Piece Cut to Waste

Fig. II.   PREPARATION

piece exactly to the shape required, so that no finishing of edges is necessary.

For cutting straight edges, a knife or razor blade, guided by a metal rule, may be used, and some simple outline shapes may be cut with a knife or pair of scissors. It will be found best to practise all the cutting methods on odd scraps of material before attempting the work of making a picture, and the complete process of making a marquetry picture is described in detail in the following chapter.

CHAPTER VI

Making a Picture: Working methods and sequence — specimen design — selection of woods — veneers used — thicknesses — preparing the design — cutting the parts to shape — use of tools — fitting and trimming — assembly — backboard — glueing — padding and cramping — framing — cleaning up — finishing.

MAKING A PICTURE

In this chapter, the complete process of making a marquetry picture is fully described, to consolidate the previous instructions, and to present the working methods in their correct sequence. The first thing to do is to prepare the design, and this may be an original, or one adapted from a print or drawing. A simple marquetry picture design for the beginner is illustrated in Fig. 12. This cliff-top scene requires eight different kinds of wood, to provide the colouring for details. In the specimen design (which may be enlarged as previously described), in order to indicate the types of wood used in the different parts of the picture, parts of the design are given a key number as shown below the illustration.

It should be appreciated that these woods are suggested as being suitable for this particular picture, and may be changed for other woods, to suit the individual. In the cliff-top picture described in the illustration, lime may be used for the sky, elm for the sea, boxwood to represent the sand, with hollywood for the cliffs, and jarrah for the rocks. The ground of the cliff-top may be myrtle and the trees walnut and violetwood. It is not essential to use the exact woods mentioned to make up the picture. For instance, cherrywood could be used instead of boxwood for the sand, beech in place of holly for the cliffs, and the trees could be walnut and blackwood.

The features in the practice picture are bold, to assist the worker, and they offer full scope for the good use of figuring and grain textures of the veneers, to provide depth of perspective. The design should be drawn full size on paper and it is suggested, if the picture is to be repeated many times, that the original should be drawn on oiled parchment paper.

Fig. 12. PRACTICE DESIGN

1 Obeche, 2 Boxwood, 3 Elm, 4 Ekki, 5 Myrtle, 6 Greenheart, 7 Walnut, 8 Violetwood

After outlining the design, the parts should be coloured to assist in the selection of the wood veneers. In selecting the veneers, care should be taken to choose woods of the same thickness, so far as is possible, and after the veneers have been chosen, they may be numbered with the same key numbers shown in the diagram, to identify them later with the parts on the picture for which they are to be used. When the veneers have been selected, all the lines of the picture should be pierced, by pricking holes with a needle, as close together as possible, as described previously in these instructions. Special care should be taken in pricking corners and small parts, to ensure that the outlines are clean, and when this has been done, the outlines of all the different parts of the work should be transferred to pattern paper, using bitumen powder pounced through the holes in the design paper, as described in the previous chapter. This part of the work should be done carefully to ensure that accurate patterns, with clean-cut outlines, are prepared, and when this has been done and the lines finished by heating the paper, the pattern parts should be glued to the selected veneers with a very thinly mixed glue, ensuring that the grain formation of the wood is used to its best advantage.

If several of the same kind of picture are to be made at the same time, the veneers with pattern papers attached should be lightly pinned to other pieces of veneers, as described in the previous instructions. When this has been done, the parts are ready to cut to shape.

Straight lines may be cut with a knife or razor blade, guided by a straight edge, with the veneers resting on a working board. The curved parts are best cut with a very fine fretsaw, with the veneers firmly held on the "v" shaped cutting table. The importance of holding the saw and other cutting tools perfectly upright when cutting the veneers to shape, cannot be over-emphasized. The saw cuts should be made very close to the line; only a *very* fine black outline should be left round the part being cut to shape. The seagull in the top left of the picture should be cut to shape from the main piece of the sky, and a small hole should be drilled in the waste to permit entry of the saw blade.

As the parts are cut to shape, they should be separated into groups, so that when the cutting out has been completed, each group of parts is sufficient to make a complete picture, and all the pictures can be made up at the same time.

For small parts of the work, and for handling brittle veneers, it is best to use a pair of tweezers when assembling the parts. All the parts of the picture should be placed in position on the original design first, to check for fitting, and any necessary trimming should be done, to ensure that each piece fits tight to its neighbours. In a well-cut piece of work, little or no trimming should be required. If trimming is necessary, it can be done by rubbing the edges *gently* with a very fine grade of glass-paper, or a shaped needle file, or by trimming with a sharp knife. The picture should be assembled methodically, and it is best to develop a fixed sequence, by working from the top left corner of the picture, across the top to the right corner, and continuing down and across the design.

When the parts of the picture have been assembled on the original design to check for fitting, the backboard can be prepared. The backboard, of plywood or hard-board, should be slightly larger all round than the picture, to allow for framing or attaching an edge of veneer. It should be appreciated that when veneers are attached to a backboard, they may tighten in drying, and pull the backboard out of shape. To counteract this, it is advisable to glue a sheet of inexpensive veneer on the reverse side of the backboard, before attaching the parts of the picture to the front, and, to ensure firm cohesion, it will be found advisable to score the backboard with a toothed plane, though this is not essential.

The outline of the edge of the picture should be marked on the backboard and, with the foundation prepared, the parts of the picture can be affixed to the base. It will be necessary to apply the glue fairly thickly in order to take up the inequalities of thicknesses, which is almost certain to occur with the use of different types of veneers. When the glue has been applied to the foundation, the parts of the picture should be transferred, piece by piece from the design, placing them on the backboard in the same sequence as before, commencing at the top left corner, and working across and down the picture from left to right. This part of the work should be done quickly and methodically, and when the veneer shapes have been laid on the glued backboard, the face of the work should be warmed, then covered with a pad made up of several thicknesses of folded newspaper, and this in turn should be covered with a thick substantial board.

With this in position, "G" cramps should be brought into use at the sides of the picture in the corners, and the work should be tightly clamped together, as illustrated in Fig. 13. When adjusting the screws of the cramps, each one should be given a half turn, working in rotation, rather than completely tightening each cramp in turn, to ensure that the level of the picture is not disturbed by cramping one side more than the other.

The object of the newspaper pad is to take up the inequality of thickness between the different veneers, so that the face of the picture will be flat. When the work has been cramped up, it should be left for the glue to chill and set for at least twelve hours. The cramps and cramping board should then be removed, to finish the marquetry picture.

The picture may be framed with strips of veneer, as illustrated

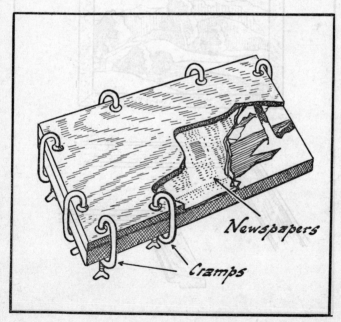

Fig. 13. HOLDING THE PARTS TOGETHER

in Fig. 14, neatly mitred at the corners, or with moulding, as shown in the illustration. Any surplus glue at the edges of the marquetry picture should first be removed, and the border cleaned off, before the framing is done. The moulding or veneer frame should be firmly and neatly glued in position, and the edges of the backboard should be trimmed. These may also be covered with strips of veneer, if it is considered necessary.

Several days—four, if possible—should be allowed to elapse,

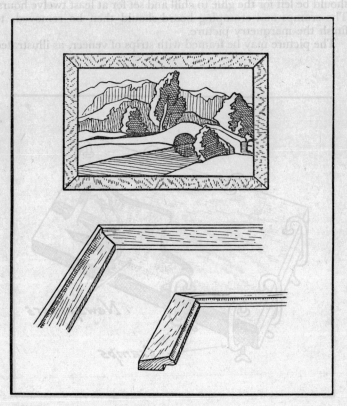

Fig. 14. FRAMING

before the picture is cleaned up, preparatory to polishing. Any scraps of the paper pad adhering to the surface of the picture should be carefully removed. Although these pieces, which adhere because of seepage of glue through the joining edges of the parts of the picture, may be dampened with water, this should not be overdone, or the water may discolour the veneers. In most cases, it will be found best to remove scraps of paper with a wood scraper, which should be very sharp. It should be appreciated that because of the thinness of the veneers, care should be taken not to remove too much of them during the cleaning up process.

To continue, a fine grade of glass-paper should be used to rub the work down. The glass-paper should be wrapped over a piece of wood which should be perfectly flat on the face side, and the grade of glass-paper used for the first rubbing down should not be coarser than Grade O. The glass-paper should be worked in the same direction throughout the rubbing down, and it will be found best to work the glass-paper block backwards and forwards along the length of the picture. The final rubbing down should be done with a finer grade of glass-paper No. OO, and, when this has been done, the dust formed by rubbing down should be removed, by brushing the work before it is finished.

The pictures can be completed by waxing or French polishing. If a wax finish is to be applied, it will be found advisable to coat the work with at least two coats of white French polish, before applying the wax.

CHAPTER VII

Alternative method of making a Picture: Description
— preparation and design — selection of veneers — pattern
making — use of key numbers — identification of grain directions in assembly — making the pad — how the layers are
arranged — saw-rag and waste pieces — simple rules of procedure — fastening the pad — saw-entry holes — use of tools —
sorting — assembling the picture — use of tape — preparation
of backboard — finishing. Another practice design — veneers
used.

ALTERNATIVE METHOD OF MAKING A PICTURE

THE method described in the previous chapter, of making a
marquetry picture is a simple one, by which some very fine work
may be done, provided care is exercised in the preliminary stages,
and the cutting out of the parts is performed carefully. It is not
the only way of making a picture, and an alternative and more
advanced method is described in this chapter. In this alternative
method, all the selected veneers are placed together—rather in
the form of a large sandwich—and a fine saw is used to cut the
parts to shape.

First, it is necessary to prepare a design and, to illustrate this
bulk-cutting method, a suitable design is illustrated in Fig. 15.
(An original design may be used, if preferred.) The same features
of boldness and clarity in design are applicable to this method of
work as to the method of separate cutting. In the design illustrated, all the parts of the picture are numbered and a key,
indicating the kinds of woods suitable for the different features,
is given beneath the drawing.

The veneers named are suggestions only, and may be changed
to suit the individual. In the specimen design, ash is suggested as
being suitable for the sky, sycamore may be used to represent the
mountains. Kingwood and boxwood for the ground, and ebony
for the river. The trees and bushes could be fashioned from
acajou, acacia, bubinga, cherrywood, birch and walnut, as indi-
cated in the key to the picture. Any suitable alternatives to these
named woods may be used, to suit the taste of the worker.

The design should be drawn full size, as previously described

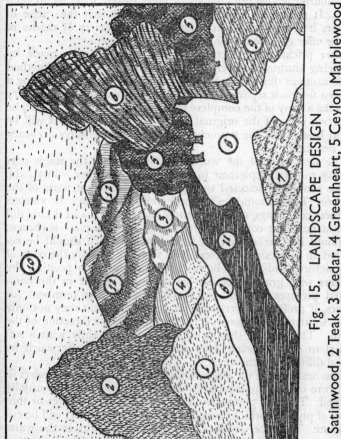

Fig. 15. LANDSCAPE DESIGN

1 Satinwood, 2 Teak, 3 Cedar, 4 Greenheart, 5 Ceylon Marblewood
6 Australian Walnut, 7 African Mahogany, 8 Boxwood, 9 Obeche
10 Ash, 11 Ebony, 12 Walnut

in the instructions, and if it is intended to preserve the design for future use, it will be found best to use oiled parchment paper. After outlining all the design features, the design picture should be coloured before pricking small holes closely together in each line. It should, of course, be remembered that the range of colours is somewhat limited, although the variety of shades of colour offer good scope for imaginative treatment.

After pricking the picture, pattern copies can be made by pouncing bitumen powder through the small holes. The method is the same as that previously described, but instead of making a pattern for each separate part of the picture,it is only necessary to make a copy of the complete picture. This could, of course, be a carbon copy of the original but, for most purposes, it will be found best to use the pouncing method which ensures accuracy and neatness.

The next part of the work is different from the single-part cutting method explained in the previous chapter. First, the woods should be selected to represent the different parts of the picture. These should be chosen carefully, selecting the veneers for their colourings, grain markings and textures, and taking full advantage of the condition of figuring. As each piece is chosen, it should be marked with a key number, which should be repeated on the design pictures. This serves to identify the parts of the picture, and it will be found a good plan to position the veneers with grain directions as they will appear in the completed pictures. Then mark the identification numbers (or letters, if preferred,) vertically in position, so that they not only serve to identify the parts, but also indicate the direction of the grain. The veneers should only be marked lightly with a soft pencil to avoid scoring deep marks which may afterwards be found difficult to remove.

The next part of the work consists of assembling the veneers in the form of a many-layered sandwich or "pad", as it is usually termed. The first piece should be an inexpensive veneer or thin sheet of plywood which, because of the rag of the saw, will be cut to waste. Then the woods selected should be laid over the waste piece, arranging them piece by piece, and layer by layer, so that the grain of each piece will be running in the direction in which it will be required in the finished picture.

This will obviously require some thought in execution, and by studying the specimen design, it will be appreciated that it is not necessary to form a separate layer for each type of wood used in the picture, or for each separate part of the design. Many of the pieces can be arranged to form a single layer in the pad, provided some general rules are followed, and that there are no very great differences of thicknesses between the veneers. Here are the rules:

1. No joining pieces of the picture should be arranged in a single layer.
2. Each layer of the pad should be filled in as much as possible, by using waste pieces to fill any gaps.
3. It is essential that each edge of a part to be cut, should be supported by a piece of waste veneer, or another part of the picture, to eliminate damage through the drag of the saw.
4. The top layer should be a complete piece of veneer.

To fully appreciate these simple rules, study the picture, Fig. 15. After the waste piece has been laid down, the parts numbered two, three, six and seven could be arranged in the first layer, and when the empty patches of the layer have been filled in with waste pieces left over from other work, the next layer could be formed of the veneers for the parts numbered eight (in the foreground), five (right of tree), twelve (right), four and eleven, with the next layer of veneers numbers nine, five (left of tree), and one, leaving numbers twelve (left) and eight, for the next layer. The top layer should consist of the piece for the sky (numbered ten in the illustration), which should be a complete layer of that particular veneer.

Before the top layer of the pad is placed in position, the full pattern made from the original pricked design should be glued to the piece and placed on the pad, which should look like the one illustrated in Fig. 16. When all the parts of the pad have been assembled, the layers should be clamped together, then fastened with fine veneer pins, through waste parts of the woods (the points of the pins should be nipped off, to prevent splitting), or adhesive paper or plastic tape may be used to hold the layers of the pad together, as illustrated in Fig. 17.

Also in the illustration, Fig. 17, are shown some small holes in the marginal edge of the picture, and it will be seen that these are positioned where an outline in the design meets the edge of the picture. The small holes which should be cut with a small

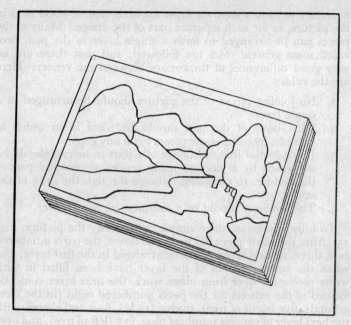

Fig. 16.   MULTIPLE CUTTING

drill, are provided to permit entry of the saw blade before it is secured in the frame. If there are any small inset pieces in parts of the picture, such as the bird illustrated in Fig. 12, in the top left corner, a saw-entry hole should be drilled exactly on the outline of the part, and preferably in a corner.

It will be appreciated that the drill should be held perfectly upright while the hole is being cut, also in sawing it is essential that the blade be kept upright. If this is not done, the parts of the picture will fit badly together. Use the "v" table when sawing, keeping the blade moving in the one direction only, and moving the pad as the pattern outline changes direction. No attempt should be made to force the saw into the work or the blade may snap. The blade should be so adjusted that the sawing action is effective on the downward stroke.

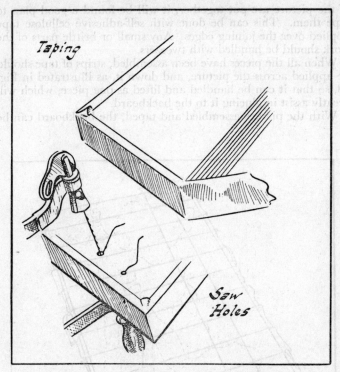

Fig. 17. TAPING AND SAWING

As the pieces are cut to shape, they should be sorted, separating the veneer parts of the picture from the waste pieces. All the waste pieces should be carefully saved. Usually, even very small pieces can be put to good use in making other pictures. The straight edges of the picture should be cut through with a fine-toothed tenon saw, to complete this part of the work.

The next part of the work consists of fitting the parts of the picture together, and this is best done on the original design. Commence, as previously described, in the top left corner, and work across and down the picture. Place each part in position, carefully trimming any joining edges, if necessary. As the parts of the picture are put together, it will be found a good plan to tape them. This can be done with self-adhesive cellulose tape applied over the joining edges. Any small or brittle parts of the work should be handled with tweezers.

When all the pieces have been assembled, strips of tape should be applied across the picture, and down it, as illustrated in Fig. 18, so that it can be handled and lifted as one piece, which will greatly assist in glueing it to the backboard.

With the picture assembled and taped, the backboard can be

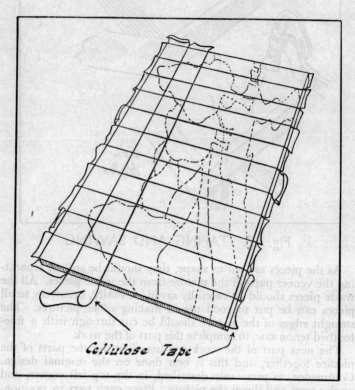

Cellulose Tape

Fig. 18. HOLDING VENEERS TOGETHER

prepared. The backboard material should be of good quality, and of a size and thickness suited to the purpose to which the completed picture will be put, and it should be larger all round than the picture, to allow for fitting a frame or border. To counteract the pull of the veneer picture on the face of the board, a piece of veneer should be glued to the back of the board, and to effect good cohesion, it will be found best to tooth both sides of the board.

With this done, the outline of the picture should be clearly marked on the backboard, and a coating of glue should be applied liberally, while hot. If the glue is applied thickly, it should take up any inequalities of thickness of the different veneers used. As soon as the glue is tacky, the taped picture should be laid carefully into position on the backboard, with the taped side uppermost and, when this has been done, a pad of several folds of newspaper should be placed in position over the work. This, in turn, should be covered by a strong board, and cramps should be used to clamp the parts firmly together. When tightening the cramps, each one should be given a small adjustment in turn, to ensure that pressure is gradually and evenly applied over all the picture, and with the work cramped up, it should be left for the glue to chill and harden for at least twelve hours.

The next part of the work consists of cleaning the edges of the backboard, removing any surplus glue, and edging the picture with shaped wood moulding or strips of veneer, neatly mitred in the corners. Also, the sides of the boards should be covered with strips of veneer, and when this has been done, the work should be put aside and left for at least four days, before finishing the picture.

To finish the picture, remove any small particles of tape or paper with a very sharp wood scraper or a stiff razor blade, then the veneers should be rubbed smooth with a fine grade of glasspaper, finishing with a very fine flour grade, before it is waxed and polished. (The finishing processes are described in full in following chapters.) Although this method of cutting veneered pictures is a little more complicated than the one previously described, it will be found a very efficient method for making fine pictures, and after a little practice the marquetry worker will soon gain skill in handling the tools, and in appreciating the possibilities and limitations of the materials.

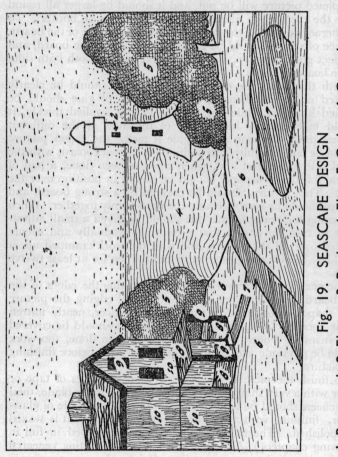

Fig. 19.   SEASCAPE DESIGN

1 Boxwood, 2 Ebony, 3 Poplar, 4 Elm, 5 Cedar, 6 Greenheart,
7 Iroko, 8 Ekki, 9 Purplewood, 10 Cherrywood

Another design for pictorial marquetry is illustrated in Fig. 19. This contains rather more detail than those previously described, but it should not be beyond the capabilities of the beginner. As with the other pictures described, the one illustrated in Fig. 19 has key numbers of the various parts of the picture, and under the picture are given the names of the woods suitable for use. These, of course, may be varied to suit the taste of the individual worker. In the picture illustrated, poplar is used for the sky, and madrona could represent the sea, and courbaril and boxwood for the paths, road and ground. The trees and the bushes could be represented with cedar and mahogany. Cherrywood and purplewood are used for the house. The lighthouse in the picture shown could be of laurel, with holly windows. Several alternatives will, no doubt, suggest themselves to the marquetry worker, and after making the simple picture illustrated the worker should be able to progress to more advanced designs.

As in all branches of craftwork, it is necessary to spend some time in practice, before possibilities of the craft can be fully appreciated. In pictorial marquetry there is great scope for the use of imagination in design and application.

CHAPTER VIII

Finishing Processes: Smoothing and polishing — types of treatment — care in preliminary stages — filling cracks — use of Beaumontage — making the stopping — colouring — grain filling — use of polishes. **French Polishing:** White polish — ingredients and mixing — grooved cork — making a fad — charging the fad — sequence of movements — first coats — building up the groundwork — treatment of blemishes — making a rubber — the rubber in use — sequence of movements.

FINISHING PROCESSES

THESE are very similar to those employed in finishing solid work. Most forms of veneered work are polished, and the true beauty of wood veneers cannot be fully appreciated until they have been smoothed and polished, which gives them depth and life. Polishing can be done with wax or French polish, or the veneered picture may be treated with oil, or varnished.

It must always be appreciated, in finishing the work, that the treatment is being applied on a thin layer of wood only—wood veneers which vary in density and porosity, which rest on a bed of glue. Incidentally, if the veneers are very thin, the glue may seep through and stain them. Success in finishing is largely due to the exercise of care in the preliminary stages of the work, in ensuring that all the parts of a marquetry picture fit neatly together, and letting any inequalities in the thicknesses of the veneers be taken up in the glue space, so that the surface of the picture is perfectly flat.

After rubbing down with a flour grade of glass-paper, the next step in progression is to fill any large cracks between the joining edges of parts of the picture, and this is best done with a type of wood stopping which is known as beaumontage. Beaumontage can be made by the home marquetry worker from equal parts of crushed resin and beeswax. The beeswax should be shredded and mixed with the resin, then heated in a tin until the two ingredients are completely dissolved and thoroughly mixed. Care should be taken not to overheat the mixture, which is inflammable. While it is still liquid, the mixture should be poured on to a flat tin lid, and when it is almost set, it should be rolled between the palms

56

of the hands to form it into a stick, and it should then be laid aside to harden.

In use, the stick of stopping material should be melted with a small heated tool, so that the beaumontage melts and runs into the cracks between the wood. It should be built up slightly higher than the actual joins being filled, as it shrinks slightly in setting; and after it has hardened, the beaumontage may be levelled by scraping it with a stiff razor blade, then finishing with a very fine grade of glass-paper. It will be necessary to colour the beaumontage, for use with woods of different colours, and powder colours are suitable for this purpose. The powders should be mixed into the beaumontage when it is melted from the stick as the cracks are being filled.

A grain filler should be used to fill the grain of the wood. It should be appreciated that a filler is not a stopping and should only be used for filling any very small inaccuracies, due to the difference of the various levels of the grain fibres. The use of the filler should not be over-done.

The veneers should not be stained, to gain the required colours, and the object in this part of the work is to bring out the natural tones of the wood. The composition of colouring of a picture is a matter for consideration in the preliminary stages of the work, and not during the finishing processes. If the work is to be finished by French polishing, do not use button polish, garnet polish or orange polish, which will discolour the work. Only white French polish should be used, and this can be made by the home marquetry worker, by dissolving six to eight ounces of bleached shellac in one pint of methylated spirits. The mixture should be kept tightly sealed when it is not being used.

FRENCH POLISHING

The complete process of French polishing is explained in great detail in the book, *Wood Finishing*,* which is another in the Foyles Series of Handbooks, and the following information is condensed from that book, for the marquetry worker who wishes to give the picture a professional finish. After mixing the ingredients mentioned above, the polish should be left until it has completely dissolved, and this may take several days. During this time, the bottle should be shaken occasionally. The marquetry worker

* *Wood Finishing*. By W. A. G. Bradman. (2s. 6d.)

will find it best to make his own polish, although some quite good proprietary brands of polish are obtainable. When the polish is being used, an additional cork will be required. This should have a fairly deep v-shaped groove cut in it, to assist in controlling the flow of the polish, so that the pad, which is known professionally as a "fad" is not overloaded.

Some wadding will be required for making fads and rubbers, and it will be found best to use unbleached wadding, as bleached wadding or medicated cotton wool is not entirely suitable for this purpose. When bleached wadding or medicated cotton wool are soaked in polish, they usually pack into a hard mass and are completely unresponsive to small changes in the pressure of the fingers and hands made during the polishing operations.

The fad, which is illustrated in Fig. 20, is a piece of wadding, folded into the shape of a pear. To make the fad, cut an eight inch square of wadding from a sheet, soak the square in the prepared polish, and leave it to dry. This preliminary soaking will ensure that any loose surplus fluff is soaked into the main body of the wadding, and will not come loose during use.

The fad should then be re-softened with a little methylated spirit, and any surplus squeezed out. With this done, the sheet of wadding should be folded in half across its width, and then three times triangularly, as illustrated in Fig. 20. When the sequence of folding has been completed, the fad should be shaped with the fingers to form the finished pear shape, as shown in the illustration.

To use the prepared fad, some polish should be poured on to it, and it should be made fairly wet, but not too wet. The fad should not drip with polish and, when squeezed lightly between the fingers, the polish should exude from the fad but should not run out of it. With this done, tap the sole of the fad several times on a piece of brown paper to flatten it, and evenly distribute the polish throughout.

At this stage of the work, no cover is required, and the charged fad is used straight on the wood. As the polish is used and the fad needs recharging, this can be done by pouring more polish on from the bottle, or by dipping the fad into polish which has been poured into a shallow tin lid. This dipping of the fad is only used in the preliminary stages of the work. The object of using the fad is to ensure that the veneers are completely sealed in preparation for the subsequent stages of the polishing. No oil

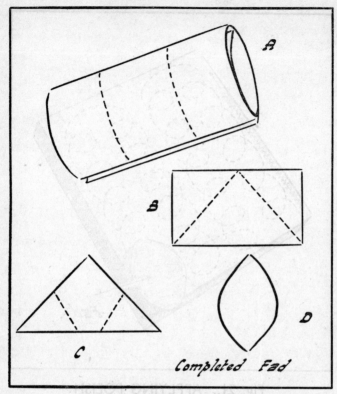

A

B

C

D

Completed Fad

Fig. 20. MAKING A FAD

should be used on the rubber during application of the first two or three coats of the polish or it may be trapped in the pores of the wood beneath the layers of shellac. If oil is used, it may work its way out to the surface of the polish, causing cracks and spoiling the finish. The fad should be worked backwards and forwards across the work, covering every part of the picture and applying the coat of polish as evenly as possible. If the fad needs recharging, it should be dipped or recharged as described above, but the amount of polish should not be excessive, or streaks or ridges of wet polish may harden on the surface of the work.

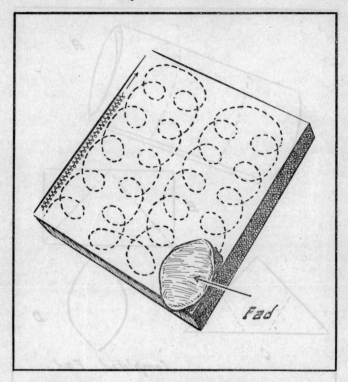

Fig. 21.   APPLYING POLISH

The first coat of French polish dries out very quickly, and when it is dry, the surface of the veneer picture should then be lightly rubbed down with a very fine grade of glass-paper to remove any traces of filler which may have worked through the coating of polish.   The process of coating and rubbing down should be repeated at least twice, to ensure that the veneers are properly sealed.

The next part of the work consists of building up a groundwork of polish, and in this part of the process, it will be necessary to use oil to lubricate the fad.   For marquetry work, a white mineral oil will be found the most suitable lubricant. It should be appreciated that throughout all the work of polishing, the oil is used as a lubricant only and, after polishing has been completed, it has to be removed; therefore the use of oil should not be excessive.

To continue, charge the fad and shake a few drops of oil on the surface of the work, then work the fad over the wood, collecting the scattered oil and spreading it evenly over the face of the work. If necessary, a little more oil can be added, to ensure that the whole surface of the veneered picture is covered. During this part of the work, the fad should be moved over the picture in the longest direction, and when the work has been completely covered with oil, it will show dull when viewed held level with a light.

The movement of the fad should then be changed, to work it in fairly large circles, as illustrated in Fig. 21. The bulk of the work should be covered in circles and the extreme edges should be coated, by manipulating the fad to form small figures of eight, as shown in the illustration, Fig. 21. At this stage of the work, pressure on the fad should be strengthened, but if any bright streaks show on the surface of the work when a newly charged fad is used, a little oil should be applied to the surface of the picture, and the work continued. When it can be observed that the layer of polish is being built up on the surface of the wood, the movement of the fad should be changed to cover the work with large flat figures of eight, as illustrated in Fig. 22. At the extreme edges, the work should be covered with very small continuous circles, as shown in the illustration.

At this stage of the process, the object is to spread the polish evenly over the surface of the veneer picture, and the effectiveness of this can be judged by the oily smear. The surface of the work should have a dull matt finish, and the path of the fad should be clearly seen. Any blemishes on the polish which are formed by particles of fluff and loose dust settling on the surface of the work, should be lightly rubbed down with a piece of very fine glass-paper which has been lightly smeared with oil. This completes the first stage of the work, and the fad can now be dispensed with.

The next part of the work is done with a rubber, and this is simply a wadding fad covered with material. To make a rubber, cut a piece of wadding eight inches square, and fold it as in making a fad. Charge the fad with polish, pouring it on the back,

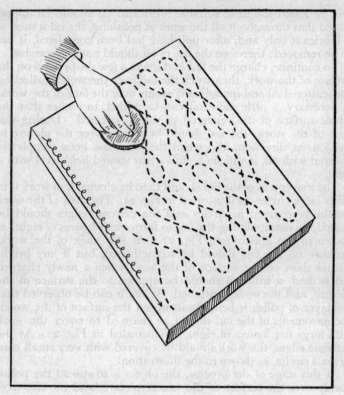

Fig. 22. MOVEMENT OF FAD

and then cover it with cloth. The best type of fabric to use is a washed out linen handkerchief or some similar material, which must be completely free of fluff and loose strands. Coloured fabrics are not suitable for use as rubber covers.

There is a correct way of covering the rubber, and this is illustrated in Fig. 23. The complete rubber should have a smooth surface on the underside. It should be quite free from wrinkles and it should be folded in such a way as to preserve the pear shape. It is not sufficient merely to cover the wadding with cloth and screw this up, as this will only have the effect of making the

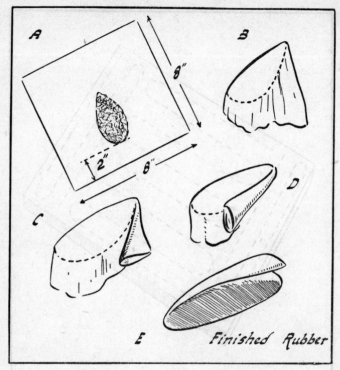

Fig. 23. MAKING A RUBBER

contacting surface into a disc which will decrease the effective size of the rubber. Also, in use, the polish will exude at the edges of the disc, which will become more heavily charged than the main part of the rubber, and may leave streaks of polish on the work.

To make a cover, cut a piece of the selected material into a square of about eight inches wide, and place the prepared wadding on the square of material, as illustrated in Fig. 23. Hold the rubber with the left hand, as shown in the illustration and, with the fingers of the right hand, press the point of the wadding up to the cloth and at the same time draw it tight over the face. Then

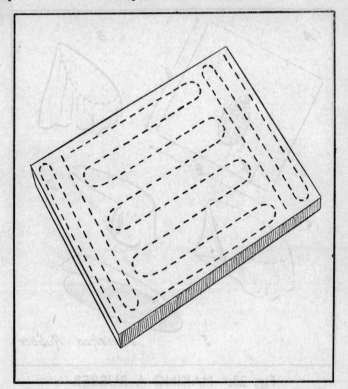

Fig. 24.   DIRECTION OF RUBBER MOVEMENTS

hold the point of the rubber lightly between the fingers of the right hand, and fold the covering material back from the point as shown. Fold the covering again, so that the edge lies along the side of the rubber, then hold the front part of the cloth over the pad, with the loose material tucked under the thumb. With this done, twist the rubber round in the hand, in an anti-clockwise direction, to wrap the material firmly round, but ensure that the flat surface of the rubber is preserved. When completed, the rubber should be charged with polish, and a little oil should be rubbed into the work, using the rubber as shown in Fig. 22.

Fig. 25. DIRECTION OF FINISHING

The application of oil is renewed so that the shellac may dry out evenly. Fold a fresh cover over the rubber and recharge it, then apply a coating of polish, as illustrated in Fig. 24, using the rubber very lightly, and working it backwards and forwards across the work, finishing the ends as shown in the illustration. The rubber should not be recharged with polish until it is nearly dry. The finishing strokes should be made as shown in Fig. 25, to take the rubber straight up and down the picture, completely leaving the wood at both ends. At this stage of the work, the rubber should be glided over the surface so that any excess polish is not scraped off the rubber, to form a hard ridge, by the edges

3

of the picture. This coating of polish should be left to thoroughly
harden before the next part of the work is done. The next step is
known as bodying, and it will be described in the following
chapter.

CHAPTER IX

French Polishing: Bodying — building up the thickness — rubber pull — description of process — lubrication and friction — charging the rubber — sequence of movements — removal of oil — building up. Methods of finishing — spiriting off — sequence of work— use of a spirit rubber. Stiffing — sequence and purpose — blemishes and faults.

FRENCH POLISHING

THE next part of the work of French polishing marquetry pictures is known as "bodying" and consists of building up an appreciable thickness of a clear and even film of shellac. This is one of the most important parts of the process, and unless it is properly done, a good finish cannot be obtained.

During bodying, the pull on the rubber is important, and the way in which the polish is being applied to the work is determined by the amount of pull evident between the rubber and the face of the work. To appreciate this, it is necessary to explain that the polish consists of two ingredients, shellac and methylated spirit, to which is added oil. In its final state, French polish is merely a film of shellac spread on evenly over the surface. As the spirits have evaporated and the oil is removed it would, of course, be possible to completely dispense with the oil and merely brush on a mixture of spirit and shellac, but in doing so it would not be possible to lay on the film of shellac evenly which is essential to good quality work and, for this reason, brush polishes are never superior to the finish of a French polished surface.

Although in preparing the polish it may appear that the shellac has completely dissolved, in actual fact, the polish is composed of small soft particles of shellac which have to be spread flat over the surface of the wood, merging with neighbouring particles to produce a solid film of polish. The shellac is sticky and soft, and so long as there is a fair amount of spirit in the polish, the rubber will slide easily over the shellac, but as soon as the spirit has evaporated, all that is left is a thin film of shellac which, if friction is applied, will become a tacky mess. There must, of course, be a certain amount of friction, or the shellac cannot be

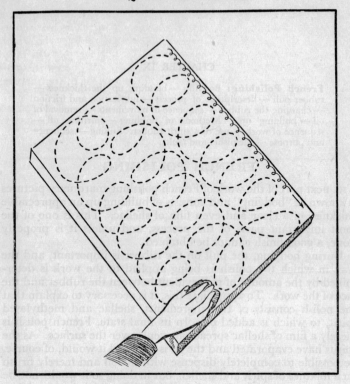

Fig. 26. BODYING MOVEMENTS

spread easily. Therefore, it is the amount of friction applied in French polishing which is the important factor, and the only method of judging the friction is by the pull of the rubber. When the pull is too great, due to evaporation of the spirit, the shellac may easily be pulled into a lumpy surface, and to avoid this happening, oil is used as a lubricant. The oil does not, of course, mix with the spirit or the shellac, but merely acts as a lubricant, and prevents working the shellac into humps.

The rubber should be charged so that it exudes polish when the sole is pressed, but it should not drip drops of polish for, when the rubber is used, the sweep of polish which it leaves should not have clearly defined edges, or ridges may be built up. The first movements of the bodying process are illustrated in Fig. 26, which shows how the rubber is worked over the surface to form large circles. The edges of the work should be worked over with small circles. It is important to cover the entire surface of the picture, paying special attention to edges and corners.

The pressure of the rubber should be increased as the polish becomes used, and the rubber should be worked until it is nearly

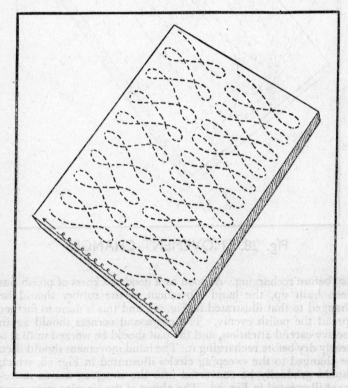

Fig. 27. MOVEMENT CHANGES

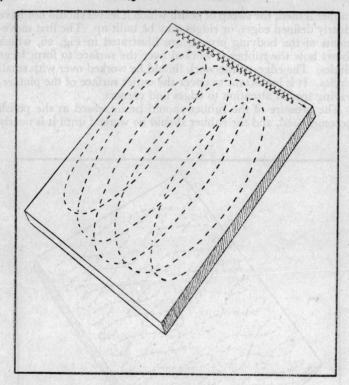

Fig. 28.　MOVEMENT CHANGES

dry before recharging. As soon as a good thickness of polish has been built up, the hand movement of the rubber should be changed to that illustrated in Fig. 27, and this is done to further spread the polish evenly. The edges and corners should again receive careful attention, and the pad should be worked until it is nearly dry before recharging it. The hand movement should then be changed to the sweeping circles illustrated in Fig. 28, which should gradually be converted into the sweeping across movement illustrated in Fig. 29. The object of the circular movement is to pull over the polish which, when laid lengthwise with the

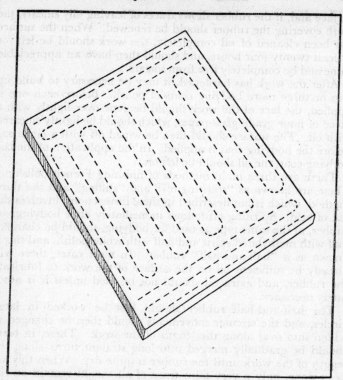

Fig. 29. FINISHING MOVEMENTS

picture, tends to form into ridges. The progressive movement of the rubber smooths out the ridges to present a smooth surface, and these ridges should be rubbed out as soon as they become apparent in the work.

The last stage of bodying is to go over the surface of the work with a new rubber, and without using any oil. The rubber should be taken up and down the length of the work, and it should only be very lightly charged with polish. The object is to remove the oil from the surface of the work. This should be done with the work placed convenient to a light, so that it reflects on the surface and, if the rubber shows traces of leaving oily smears, the cloth covering the rubber should be renewed. When the surface has been cleaned of oil completely, the work should be left for at least twenty-four hours, and should then have an appreciable shine and be completely free from smears.

After the work has hardened, it may be necessary to build up two or three more bodying coats of polish. Before each one is applied, the face of the work should be gone over lightly with a piece of flour grade glass-paper, which should be lightly smeared with oil. The surface should then be wiped off with a clean rag before the bodying coat is applied. In the application of the last bodying coat, the oil should be left on.

There are three main methods of finishing French polishing. These are known as "spiriting off" and "stiffing" and the third method, which is not described in these instructions, involves the use of acid. Spiriting off follows immediately after bodying. A rubber, of the same type as used for bodying, should be charged, half with methylated spirit and half with white polish, and this is known as a "half-and-half" rubber. In most cases, there will already be sufficient oil on the surface of the work to lubricate the rubber, and extra oil should not be used unless it is absolutely necessary.

The half-and-half rubber should first be worked in large circles, and the circular movements should then be changed to widen into oval along the length of the work. These, in turn, should be gradually merged into long straight turns along the length of the work until the rubber is quite dry. When this has been done, only a very faint trace of oil should remain on the surface of the work.

To remove the final traces of oil, the work should be gone over with a spirit rubber, which will also serve to burnish the surface of the picture. The spirit rubber can be made by washing out an old rubber cover, until it is completely free of polish. With this done, the washed rubber should be used to cover a wadding pad, and the whole should then be covered with a fresh clean piece of linen. To charge the spirit rubber, a few drops of methylated spirit should be sprinkled into the palm of the hand, and the rubber dipped into it. The charging of the rubber is best tested by holding it against the lips; it should not feel wet, but cold. If the rubber is overcharged with spirits, the polish may be softened, and may be pulled up into humps when the rubber is used.

The spirit rubber should be used straight up and down the longest way of the work, and care should be taken to ensure that the complete surface is evenly rubbed. The action of the rubber should be to leave bright streaks, which indicate that the oil has been removed. Rubbing should be continued until the spirit rubber is quite dry and when the surface displays a really good gloss. For final polishing and burnishing, the spirit rubber should be dipped into some Vienna chalk, and worked up and down the surface of the veneer picture in the same way as the spiriting rubber is worked. After this has been done, the work should be laid aside for the polish to thoroughly dry and harden.

Stiffing is done rather differently from spiriting off. In stiffing, it will be found best to make a new rubber. Apply one bodying coat with it, then carry straight on with stiffing, which is done by charging the rubber with about half the amount of polish used previously for bodying, but without using any oil. The surfacing should be commenced from the far edge of the longest side of the picture, working straight over the surface over and off the ends. Each returning stroke should overlap the previous stroke, and this sequence of actions should be continued until all the work has been treated. Care should be taken to keep the rubber working in straight lines across the work, and the rubber should not be circled. The action is a gliding one, and the pull on the rubber will increase as the oil is removed. Use the rubber very lightly in the finishing stages of the work, and be careful not to overcharge it. When the surface of the marquetry picture is completely free from oil, the work should be set aside for the polish to set and thoroughly harden.

If each stage of the work has been done carefully and methodically, the finish should be completely satisfactory. Blemishes and faults are due only to insufficient care taken in one of the processes. Some common faults, and how to avoid them, are described under.

A spotty or pimply surface is one which is marred by small raised spots. These are due to small particles of dust settling on the surface of the work during treatment, and they become covered with polish which hardens. They may be removed before the finishing process, by lightly sanding them with a very fine grade of glass-paper treated with oil. Of course, the obvious way to avoid these blemishes is to work in a dust-free atmosphere.

Ridges running across the length of the work are caused by

faulty rubbing, and perhaps by overcharging the rubber. This can only be avoided by exercising care in working the sequence of rubber movements.

A streaky surface is usually caused by faulty application of the polish. It is essential in the rubbing stages to follow the sequence of movements described in the preceding instructions to evenly spread the polish over the surface of the work. The friction tension in evenly laying on the shellac is important, and it may need some practice before the "feel" of this process is gained. This fault may also be due to lack of care in filling and sealing the grain of the wood, and it should be appreciated that many different woods are used in a marquetry picture.

A dull surface appearance in the finished work is due to using too much lubrication in the form of oil, or not completely removing the oil in the final stages of the work, but after a little practice the beginner should be able to counteract this fault in the early stages of the work.

Another common fault of the beginner is the forming of white streaks, or bloom, after the work has been completed. This is due to moisture becoming entrapped under the polish, and the best way to avoid this is to work in a dry warm room. If the atmosphere is damp or humid, there is every possibility that the work may become damp. Care should be taken to ensure that the surface of the work is dry before commencing any of the polishing treatments.

The formation of very fine cracks in the work is due to the "sweating" of entrapped oil. Unless the oil is removed between each stage of polishing, it will become coated with subsequent layers of polish, and will later work its way to the surface of the work, causing fine cracks to appear in the polish. This fault is sometimes termed "Chinese writing", and it may be due to using different types of polish in the work. The same mixture of polish should be used for all the applied coats. The only way to put this fault right is to strip the work and completely re-polish it.

As in any other branch of marquetry, or other craft, practice is necessary to attain a high standard of perfection.

they are thoroughly mixed. If resin is used for hardening the wax, the amount added to the mixture should be equal to one sixth of the amount of wax.

It should be appreciated that the compound is very inflammable. It should not be heated over a naked flame, and furthermore, the turpentine should never be added to the hot wax mixture when standing near a naked flame. For all these reasons, a double-jacketed container, as described, is to be recommended, and great care should be taken to avoid the dangers outlined above.

A smooth soft rag may, from long experience, be found the best method of applying wax, but in the early stages, it is best to make up a wax pad from a piece of cotton wool, covered with a soft rag, which should be moistened with the polish.

CHAPTER X

Alternative Finishing Methods: Polishing and varnishing — making wax polish — ingredients and mixing — use of hardeners — applying wax polish — brush finish — suitable varnishes — spirit varnish — application — preparation of work — filling — applying oil varnish — smoothing down and finishing. Conclusion.

ALTERNATIVE FINISHING METHODS

FRENCH polishing, of course, is not the only method of finishing marquetry pictures, which may be varnished or wax polished, both very simple processes which are briefly explained below.

Wax polishing a picture is a very popular method, which produces an attractive eggshell gloss which can be regulated in texture, according to the amount of polish used. It will be found best to first seal the grain, as previously described, and apply at least two coats of white French polish, which will preserve the richness of the finish. A good quality wax polish should be used; some quite good proprietary brands are obtainable, or the marquetry picture maker can mix his own polish.

There are several ways of making wax polish, but the best quality for the marquetry worker is one made from a mixture of *pure* American turpentine and beeswax. If a turps substitute is used, the quality of the polish will be inferior to that mixed with pure turpentine. To harden the mixture of turps and wax, stearine wax, resin or Carnaubba wax may be added to the two main ingredients.

To make the wax, any double-jacketed container—such as a glue-pot—will be required, or a suitable vessel can be contrived from a tin suspended in a saucepan. The beeswax should be shredded into the inner container, hot water should be poured into the outer jacket, and heat applied. As the beeswax melts, the turpentine should be added—a little at a time—stirring the mixture well until it is of the consistency of thick cream. At this stage, the hardening wax, in the proportion of one part of hardener to four parts of beeswax, may be shredded and added to the mixture. The ingredients must be well stirred to ensure that they are thoroughly mixed. If resin is used for hardening the wax, the amount added to the mixture should be equal to one sixth of the amount of wax.

It should be appreciated that the compound is very inflammable. It should not be heated directly over a naked flame, and during handling, reasonable precautions should be taken to avoid the risk of fire. For marquetry pictures, where it is not desired to darken the woods, it will be found best to use bleached beeswax, and the hardener should not be one that may darken the colour of the wax.

A smooth soft rag, free from loose fluff, should be used for applying the polish. The polish may be applied quite generously to the surface of the work, and should be evenly spread. If a shaped moulding is used to frame the picture, it may be found best to apply the wax with a brush. Following application, the work should be left until the turpentine has evaporated, which may take several hours, according to the amount of polish applied. After the work has dried, the polishing should be done. A soft cloth may be used, but in most cases a better effect will be obtained by brushing the work—a shoe brush may be used, provided it is clean.

The work may require several coatings of the wax polish before a really good surface can be worked up, and furniture cream should be used as the finishing treatment to obtain a good shine.

An alternative to wax polishing is the use of varnish for finishing a marquetry picture. Spirit or oil varnish may be used; a suitable spirit varnish for coating marquetry pictures is one which is termed "bleached-white" varnish. Spirit varnishes are quick-drying and must, therefore, be applied with speed. A clean soft brush should be used and the varnish should be floated on, with the work done in a dry dust-free atmosphere. Care should be taken in applying spirit varnish to avoid brush "drag", which will be visible when the varnish has dried.

Before applying any kind of varnish, it will be necessary to prepare the work carefully. The rubbing down of the picture woods should be done some time before the varnish is applied, to allow any dust in the air to settle, and before varnishing, the work must be thoroughly dusted. The grain of the woods should be filled, or the varnish may dry unevenly, due to the difference in porosity of the woods used, and a very thin coat of glue size should be applied over the filling. When the size has dried, it should be lightly rubbed down with a very fine grade glass-paper, and the work should again be cleaned free of dust.

For applying the varnish, it will be found best to use a proper varnish brush which is bevelled at the ends of the hairs and, of course, it is essential that the brush be really clean and free from dust.

It may be necessary to apply more than one coat of oil varnish. Oil varnish is easier to apply than spirit varnish and is slower drying. The varnish should be floated on the picture, which is best laid flat and level. The work should first be covered by brushing up and down its length, then the brush should be worked across the width of the work, again lengthwise. Although the varnish may be generously applied to the work if it is level, it should not be laid on too heavily, and it will be found best to apply two or more thin coats rather than one thick coat. Between the application of each coat of oil varnish, the preceding coat, when it is dry, should be levelled by rubbing the surface with pumice powder sprinkled on a dampened piece of felt placed over a smooth wood rubbing block. The face of the work should also be dampened, and after the work has been evenly treated, it should be washed with clean cold water. The picture should be set aside to thoroughly dry before the next coat of varnish is applied. It will not, of course, be necessary to rub down the final coat of varnish.

Hanging the marquetry picture is simply a matter of fastening screw eyes or swivel hangers to the back of the picture, or if round plaques are made, a single hanger can be used as a means of suspension.

As the marquetry worker continues to progress, more intricate and difficult designs may be attempted, and as the worker becomes experienced, some very fine work can be done, particularly by effecting good perspective in a picture, by the expert selection of veneers especially suited to the purpose, by virtue of their colourings or figuring. Subtle light and shade effects will do much to bring perfection to the work, and portraiture in marquetry is quite possible, although it does require great skill in selection of the woods and their application.

As has already been explained in the Introduction, this book deals mainly with pictorial marquetry, using thin layers of fine veneers. The craft of pictorial marquetry is one that can be made a complete and satisfying hobby. It has many facets of interest, and there is good scope for imaginative progression. It is a craft of full variety, in which the work can be used for wall pictures mainly, but also for other purposes. Boxes and casket lids can be decorated with marquetry pictures, while firescreens form excellent subjects for the application of picture marquetry. Book-ends and trays are other articles which may be enriched with this form of wood decoration, and the worker in the craft will find that there is a very good market for well-executed work. By using the method previously described of using oiled paper for original designs, the pictorial marquetry worker can quickly build up a stock of designs, and so save a great deal of work in the preliminary stages.

As the craftworker progresses, the initial outfit of tools and equipment may be enlarged and improved; the addition of a power saw, for instance, would considerably speed up the work, and if the craft is being practised as a commercial venture, saving in time has a two-fold return—it increases the margin of profit on each piece of work done, and it allows the worker to increase his output. Also, as progress is made, the worker may feel the use of special tools best suited to his own style of work—many of them can be made, and indeed, many fine craftsmen in marquetry devise and make many of their own tools and appliances; for instance, very fine saw blades can be made from watch springs.

Also, if commercial interest is great, the marquetry craftworker may like to consider the use of templates. Templates are patterns of the various parts of a marquetry picture, which are made in any strong material—such as thin metal; in use, they are placed on the selected veneer, and the outlines run round with a very fine pencil. Of course, the templates would have to be very carefully made, as accuracy in marking and cutting out is essential to a high standard of work.

Marquetry, of course, is not confined to pictorial works; there are other forms, although the decoration of furniture by marquetry is not used to any great extent in modern pieces. Pure marquetry is a very skilled craft, which requires a great deal of practice before it can be practised with efficiency. The methods of designing and cutting are similar to those used in pictorial marquetry. The design, which is usually of a conventional nature, is drawn full size on thick paper, and the outline is then pricked with fine holes made very close together. Patterns are made from the master design by pouncing, as previously described, or by rubbing powder through the fine prickings, and the paper heated to fix the design. The selected veneers are placed together to make a pad, with the marquetry pattern glued to the top sheet, and a waste piece of veneer under the pad to take the rag of the saw.

Cutting the veneers is carried out with a special piece of apparatus which is known as a "donkey", and the cutting is so done that the parts of the marquetry fit very closely together. In addition to the intended marquetry, a piece of counter marquetry can be formed from the waste.

Veneers also have many other uses—too great to include in detail in a book of this size—and altogether, working with veneers of fine woods can be made a complete and interesting pastime.